Mouth Art of the Bald-faced Hornet

poems by

Betsy Bolton

Finishing Line Press
Georgetown, Kentucky

*Mouth Art of
the Bald-faced Hornet*

Copyright © 2024 by Betsy Bolton
ISBN 979-8-88838-518-0 First Edition
All rights reserved under International and Pan-American Copyright Conventions. No part of this book may be reproduced in any manner whatsoever without written permission from the publisher, except in the case of brief quotations embodied in critical articles and reviews.

Publisher: Leah Huete de Maines
Editor: Christen Kincaid
Cover Art: "Sycamore" by Randall Exon, 2023
Back Cover Art: "Crum Embankment" by Randall Exon, 2023
Author Photo: James Peyton Jones
Cover Design: Elizabeth Maines McCleavy

Order online: www.finishinglinepress.com
also available on amazon.com

Author inquiries and mail orders:
Finishing Line Press
PO Box 1626
Georgetown, Kentucky 40324
USA

Contents

Introit 1

1. Contact

Muddle 5
Unsettling 6
Colonial surveyor 7
Damsel 8
Mouth Art of the Bald-faced Hornet 9
Hoerenkill, 1631 10
Fiddlehead feint 11
First Crum mill, 1643 12
Crickets 13
Emergence 14
Water striders 15
Caleb Pusey's gristmill arrives 16
Habitat 18
Flouring of Lenapehocking 19
Hydroplaning 20
Ephemera 21
Bounded 22
Eddying 23
Invasion 24
Heartland 25
An "imperfect idea" 26
Amphibious 27
Mycorrhizae 28

2. Surfacing

Snow-melt carrion call 31

Sycamore shelter 32

Cicada courtship 33

Gunpowder, 1776 34

Fiddlehead tonic 35

Nettled 36

Ghost bowing 37

Grasped 38

The rapture 39

Buttonwood agreement, 1792 40

Metamorphosis 42

Retted 43

Plush 45

Bedrock 46

Volunteers, 1892 47

Reading the forested landscape 49

Beech 50

Dredging 51

3. Rapt

Surface tension 55

Rapture: early lessons 56

Tunnel dreams 57

Spiral 59

Writing 60

Impounded, 1931 61

Discernment 63

Jewelweed	64
Natural history	65
Repair	66
Worm sex	67
It looks like rage	68
Sanctuary	69
Heartwood	71
No fossils here	72
Insiders	73
Living fossils	74
Flood	75
Listen	76
Taste	77
Broken	78
Flight	79
Notes	81
Acknowledgments	87

Introit

Hear the call of the creek:

a small gurgle, water surprised
by the distance from rock to lower ledge;
wren tittering, the sound oscillating,
a beating wing across the Blue Route's roar.

In the beech cathedral, blue jay flashes
his sharp warning; warbler's song vaults
the sky, stirs memories—smell of leaf mold rising,
bright lemon of wood sorrel waking

the tongue. Communities converge and tesselate:
mayapple's oversized canopy borders
the toad's spiraling egg strand; trout lily blooms
where roots meet bedrock. See the cardinal turn

her eggs, nesting over peril. Groundhog pounds
in rhythmic crescendo toward a den at meadow's edge.
Long-legged boatmen scuttle the mica-silvered path,
this shimmering soil a sign of sacred ground.

Listen: here we are called to witness and wonder.

Beneath the red-bellied turtle sunning
on a partly sunken tree, a wood duck glides,
iridescent crest and mottled chestnut breast
dappled like the moving canopy's mosaic.

Beside the creek, jewelweed shapes reflecting globes
from rain and dew, each dazzling teardrop a Magnificat,
a surah, a sutra—enough to make the heart beat
double watching the sun, the world, remake itself.

Can you hear? yourself called here, present here,
reaching for a future clammy with hope,
like a salamander breathing through damp skin?
Here: yourself surrounded; inextricable; home.

I. Contact

Muddle

My first day at Crum ledge, the Crum's edge, I woke,
broke, amid longings, belongings, unbelongings,
into heat and heavy mist. On the creek beside me, a great
blue heron touched down, flapped its wide,
slow wings, pacing me down the creek until

a circle of standing stones loomed

out of the mist, the steamy meadow.
Like gravestones, buried thoughts, their words lost
to moss, to weathering: in distinct in-
vitation to anthropomorphing,
vegetalizing, insectivizing

they seemed to me, though in the end, nothing
more than a landscaping joke—leftover
construction transformed into ersatz monument—
a Crum Henge.

>   (the heron
>   a different kind of mystery)

Unsettling

Between trail and river
a lean-to:
rough-hewn
stone, a triangle

some eight feet tall,
diagonally laid
from land
to rocky outcrop.

A window on the creek.
A child's found fort.
A site we enter often
and consider ours—

until a visitor points out
the obvious:
the careful construction,
the labor of the hewing.

None of our doing.

Colonial surveyor

I dream of captured power: a creek's force
half-bound in root and land, hidden in oxbow
and sedimented plain, invisible
to the eye but there for the taking.
I calculate power from falling water,
assess flow rate and density, measure
the height of fall, local acceleration.

I dispense with dragonfly nymphs devouring
tadpoles, invertebrates and algae,
fungi, fallen leaves, bacteria
and beaver dams. The beavers are gone,
their fur turned to hats. I have no need
of the slow ribboning that makes a fertile
flood plain. I can ignore the way a creek breathes,

absorbing oxygen, releasing carbon:
midnight inhale, noon exhale; its panting
through summer heat; long slow breaths
constrained by crusts of winter ice. Only
a living being breathes. The creek is power
supply, is engine, acceleration,
lift, force, our path to the future
       —or it is nothing.

Damsel

What's in a name? Sometimes, the open
secret of how our makings bind us.

English millers imagined mill wheels
with an eye, a bosom, waist and covering skirt.

Above the wheel, a hopper delivers
grain to a "shoe." The "damsel," a spindle,

knocks against the side of the shoe to drop grain
to the eye or bosom all day long: the rapping sound,

damsel against shoe, is called the damsel's song.
When grain runs out, a strap across the hopper

strikes a bell every time the damsel knocks
the shoe: a sound called the damsel in distress.

Am I the only one who wonders,
who is kicking whom? the only one

imagining still a darker tale of a woman
knocked around, slowly ground down?

Mouth Art of the Bald-faced Hornet

A solitary queen, eggs fertilized,
half-frozen, half-hibernating through winter

in a rotting log: she wakes, alone, to build
high in the canopy. Grating wood,

forcing fiber into mouthparts, spit-balling
her palace, she flies with pelleted pulp

to the nest she builds by crawling backwards,
laying fiber, retracing, compressing, stretching

the fiber, trimming edges as she goes,
curves defined by mandibles that pinch and spread.

Once ten cells of the comb are built, she lays eggs, feeds
her larvae well-minced crane flies; they pupate, emerge.

Now the queen lays eggs only; the workers feed, guard,
build their home as an ever-growing globe

of stippled curves, walls of layered paper torn down,
remashed to reconstruct their pendulous world.

Black and white themselves, they paint in subtle shades:
sepia longings, pebbled shores, a fawn

amid the fog, chestnut tree by hazelnut,
gunmetal rattling, smoke-silvered air;

walnut tinged with slate and flint, iron and ash,
mourning dove umbered amid autumn's ochre.

Our human ears are deaf to their mouth art,
those unspoken words woven into shelter

above our heads, orchestral swelling
of the supra-organism; the soloist

hearing in the dark the harmonies she will shape
with mighty jaws: her many-faceted self, waiting

to emerge.

Hoerenkill, 1631
> *near modern-day Cape Henlopen, Delaware*

Near the mouth of great Lenapewihituck,
the corn grows tall and the Dutch divide their labor.

The Sickoneysink refuse settlers, accept
only a trading post, but Dutch ships are sparse

and the men have built a palisade, planted
corn, proclaimed a fort near Zwaanendael—

Swan valley—with a tin sign of sovereignty.
A local leader takes the Dutch sign and cuts it

to pieces to make tin pipes, the Sickoneysink
using pipes for ceremony, connection.

The Dutch complain bitterly of this aggression,
until their interlocutors provide

"clear token" of the sachem's death. Oh!
these savages! not at all what the Dutch

had wanted! Unsettled, they seek comfort
at the nearby creek they call Hoerenkill—

Whore creek—imagining both women and creek
theirs for the taking. Blind to the power

of Sickoneysink women elders, those Dutch
can't see what's coming, never perceive

themselves as abusers, to be killed as they work
in the tall corn, their settlement wiped

from the river's mouth. A well-planned attack,
no Sickoneysink injuries of note.

Dutch corporate masters forbid retaliation;
men on the next ship discover, slowly,

that Lenape women control the stores
of grain for which they hunger, reason

enough to restrain other cravings.

Fiddlehead feint

Searching for fiddleheads, I almost crush
the fern's prothallus, that tiny heart-
shaped leaf whose underside produces eggs,
plus sperm that needs water to find and fertilize

another's eggs—a drama invisible
to those of us distracted by the spirals peeking
through brown papery wrapping
as if an old-time grocer had left them,

still growing, half-packaged, on the counter.
Stiff-armed beside them, last year's fertile fronds
raise their stipes and blades, pinnae held high, enclosing
spore-bearing sori that rupture and release.

Here, says the fern: take, eat. In two moons
the real game begins, fertility emerging
inconspicuous amid the showy twice-cut
finely-dissected sterility of plume.

The first Crum mill, 1643

Flintlocks, axes, metal, woven cloth exchanged
for beaver pelts: the Lenape welcome
technology transfer, swapping innovations
of the day. A mill operates on a different scale:
transforming, terraforming. No right to build,
the sachems say. Still the new governor

insists on a mill for his New Gothenburg—
a mark of permanence, colonial success.
Inhabitants of New Sweden in 1643:
some forty men, four women, seven children,
mostly miserable—Dutch, Swedes, Finns, some English,
unable to feed themselves, almost

wholly reliant on Lenape maize.
Imagine the building: first the dam
and millrace—men breaking, bracing stone,
wedging rocks in water, wedged themselves,
woodworkers felling trees, digging sawpits,
clutching the whipsaw box and tiller

through days of fort and da, push me pull you
as they frame the building, shape the wheel.
Crazy labor to steal the lazy labor
of the creek wallowing through the woods,
the Lenape watching, bemused, impatient
for the promised trade, repeatedly delayed.

Crickets

At night, up in the oaks, true katydids divide
themselves in choirs, each internally synchronized,
but alternating with others nearby, an endless
call-and-response loud enough to have frightened

the early Pilgrims. Walking through the dark
with my children, listening to the dull roar
of the katydid choirs, I wonder what
the Wampanoag heard in the evening chorus:

psalm or praise song? insect eros? weather forecast?
My dull ears and brain can't unravel the noises
of my neighbors, though I learn online that false
katydids share songs almost as varied

as their forms: the curved tail crescendo-ing
zit-zit-ZIT like a spotty adolescent; the forked
tail practically tripping—tsip, tsip—over its own song.
Can you pick out the ground crickets? Easily mistaken,

striped, strident—they stridulate so fast, we hear
metallic chirps but not the trills beneath.
And when a person says the world must change
if we are all to survive, what does she hear

in response? Crickets, says the tired joke. As if
we ever heard them, ever noticed the pine tree
cricket hide its spruce-green wings in a tangle
of needles, its sweet song plaintive as sun

sets into night, or ever registered the spectre-
pale tree cricket trilling its interrupted aria
from the suburban dogwoods lingering
where ancient eastern forests once stood.

Emergence
          after reading Peter Sluyter and Jasper Danckaerts,
            *Journal of a Voyage to New York and a Tour
           in Several of the American Colonies in 1679-80*

I pursue, across the crumbling
translation, a world where dreamers gather,
share, contribute, combine to make a tree:

shimmering, iridescent, looming
lustrous in the dusk, more and more luminous
until from its roots a man sprouts.

The beginning of vision: to see men
as if trees, but walking. This man: a tree,
walking. No simile. Watch him pull

his soul free: first one foot shaken, then the next,
the capillary roots still clinging to his toes.
See the luster left by his first steps.

But the tree! the tree still shimmers, bends stately,
phloem, cambium, xylem, heartwood bend
until the tip touches soil, then roots, sprouts,

releases a female who draws her feet,
still rooted, from that soil. Her branching fingers
free the bowed tree, linger on its bright glow,

man and woman both dazzled and broken
by the brilliance of their first uprooting.
Watch the tree stand tall, its glimmer strengthening,

deepening, lighting the fledgling dancers
as they circle its base, knitting their branches
together into something old made wholly new.

Water striders

Skipper, skimmer, strider,
scooter, spider:
watery all;
clouds of instars
cluster on the creek
fleeing the mill paddle's rhythmic fall.

Caleb Pusey's gristmill arrives

prefabricated, on the ship from England.
Caleb's share in the venture only one-
thirty-second of the whole, but his
the managing hand, his the nose
to the stone, sniffing any risk of fire.

Chester creek floods:
twice the mill is washed away;
once it remains, damaged
so badly it must be rebuilt.
But Friends persist. Soon a sawmill

shrieks beside the gristmill.
Caleb manages his debts, doubles
his land-holdings, keeps the peace
between Friend and heathen.
Years later, the miller-philosopher recalls

> *the Indians were rather like*
> *a way of a ship in the sea*
> *which cannot be followed*
> *by any path or track*
> *that they leave behind them,*

except that they return each year
to summer residences & even two hundred fifty
years after settlers closed their land-seas behind them,
stone axes & sacred sites remain,
testifying to their tenure, showing their way.

> *All except the Indians' mostly movable*
> *settlements, was a perfect waste wilderness,*
> *the earth producing naturally to sustain*
> *the life of man no sort of grain nor fruit trees*
> *(except chestnuts)—*

except what Friends cannot recognize
as food: hickory & oak & beechnut,
ramps & great Solomon's seal,
fiddlehead ferns & nettles, shadberry
& blueberry & raspberry, besides pigeons
knocked from perches, deer trapped, shad netted.

> *When many first arrived getting what weeds*
> *or grass they could to lay under their beds*
> *got out their bed clothes to cover them*
> *with a good fire by their bedsides… they digged*
> *caves in the ground and cut down some of the trees.*

The Sharples family, for instance, live some time
beside a fallen oak, roughly sheltered with bark
and leaves. But Lenape hosts share seed corn; teach
the settlers to girdle trees and bring them down;
which plants are edible, which medicinal—

> *Seeing that the soil was good and fertile,*
> *the air mostly clear and healthy, streams of water*
> *sweet and plentiful and wood for fire and timber*
> *for building in abundance, and believing*
> *that the Lord had not inclined the hearts*
> *of so many sober people fearing his name*
> *to come over here and perish for want of food,*

wood violet, butternut bark, pine needle tea,
soft Virginia bluebells, sassafras root,
lemony wood sorrel, bright young beech leaves;
birch bark as a tonic, willow bark for pain;
witch hazel & sumac as astringents;
cattail for poultices, ginseng root for strength—

> *they kept to their meetings and on working days*
> *went cheerfully to falling trees, rooting up*
> *the roots of small shrubs, burning up what they had*
> *no occasion otherwise for and so to make way*
> *for a crop of Indian corn to be planted*
> *the next spring and till after a little time*
> *they got to ploughing and sowing of wheat*
> *of which we purpose to speak more of in the sequel.*

Habitat

See the shadowed meniscus made
by the water striders' weight and motion

as they dimple the water
without breaking molecular bonds,

those chemical connections doubled
where water meets air.

Water's surface tension,
its slippery skin,

partners in this mystery:
shaping the narrow boundary

of the strider's habitual demesne,
its divided, divisive home.

The flouring of Lenapehocking

Mills proliferate, that technology
transforming the face of Lenape land.

Listen: the millwheel plays on its harps,
each harp framed of land and furrows,

each furrow naming a relation of power:
master, journeyman, apprentice, fly.

See how each grain enters at the eye:
crossing the wheel, it is sliced, scissored

ten times by the master,
twenty by the journeyman,

the gap between wheels slowly vanishing
until only a paper's thickness remains

at the section of wheel known as the flouring
of the stone, where cracked surfaces produce

the whitest flour. See how the dressing of the wheels
mirrors the flouring of Lenape lands:

the forest and corn fields ploughed and furrowed
by the English who come pouring in, their livestock

roaming widely—roving agents of empire,
an occupying force; their crops of wheat

competing with corn, changing the soil;
their mills multiplying, diversifying,

blocking the creek at every curve and sway,
channeling, constraining the water of this shared life.

Hydroplaning

Where are you going? asks Thich Nhat Hanh,
voice wobbling through the old tape.

His question echoes through this summer morning,
the roads awash in dead and dying worms.

Slicking themselves in layers of mucus,
they hydroplane across dark tarmac, riding

the water, ignoring the underlying sharp-edged
gravel coated in poisonous tar. Caught

by daybreak, they can only dry and die,
in fluid paralysis. Scientists say that left

to themselves, worms will move less than half a mile
in one hundred years—yet here hundreds come,

breathing through their slime-coated skin,
slipping onto roads and sidewalks in the rain.

I imagine their ancestors hitching a ride with settlers,
younger generations free-surfing down the creek.

Where are you going, so impatient
on that road? asks Thich Nhat Hanh,

preparing an answer we don't want to hear.
Hydroplaning worms already know:

"We are going to death."
"Why rush?" asks the teacher.

But can the worm refuse the road?
Can we?

Ephemera

Mayapples speak
in turtle,
wrapping seeds
in sweetness
ripening
in turtle time;

the speckled
nectar
of claytonia
sings
just a moment
above the soil,

its fairy spuds
of captive sun
shaping
a long
fermata
underground.

Bounded

After less than twenty years, the people
of Crum Creek seek relief from the Friends,
"expressing great uneasiness
at the uncertainty of their settlements,"

as if the people were the new settlers, Friends
the native landholders. Crum creek families
petition the provincial council
for a "secure tract of land, bounded

in the English fashion" in order
"that they might no more live like dogs
(as they expressed themselves)." Millers move
the people—not just Caleb Pusey, an appointed

Peacemaker, but also Nate Newlin,
incorrigible peace breaker—move them
from their Crum and Ridley creek homes
to "encircled land," the Ockehocking

reservation. Five hundred acres:
less than the land then held by either Pusey
or Newlin. Meanwhile, settlers are importing
Indian slaves from the Carolinas—

so many that the provincial government,
under Iroquois threat of intervention,
bans the import (though not the practice
of slavery). Within five years a Great

Council of Indians gather at Ockehocking
to protest the growing threat of enslavement.
Encircled. Living like dogs. Lives written
on the water the millers dammed.

Eddying

Eddies:
        where a river
        turns upstream,
        runs briefly
        against its own current.

A straight-channeled creek
with pool
and riffle structure
will meander
in time
pushing pools
out to either side:
                      A sashay.
                      In time.

Pools:
        the creek
        digs deeper,
        speeds
        over the slopes
        it shapes,
        lifts pebbles
        up its micro-mountains.

        Riffles:
                the pebble drops.
                Deposition zone.
                Mid-channel:
                shallow
                sparkling
                friction.

Eddies:
        amid
the speed,
slowing,
circling,
swelling.
                This eddy:
                            A swirl.
        A pose.
                A breath.

Invasion

Through drying skin, salamanders struggle
to breathe; millipedes, mites, sowbugs disappear,
and trillium, mayflower, lady's slippers vanish.

Pleistocene glaciers killed all earthworms here,
but after millennia, non-native species hitched a ride
with non-native humans bringing plants, soil,

ship's ballast to discard, including a hunger
of earthworms whose plantations may outlive
imperial human holdings aboveground.

Even trees and nesting birds lose ground.
piles of petioles—the stems of leaves—
mark the burrows of *Lumbricus terrestris:*

worms pull in and eat the leaves, push out their castings,
industrious, practically industrial.
Other signs of dis-ease: trees whose roots flare

as soil shrinks, erodes, dries, withholds bounty—
leaving root crowns exposed in this land bereft
of ground cover. Of course the worm turns,

of course we close our eyes: now what end to empire?
Close your eyes still tighter and follow underground
the salamander's slither, the sowbug's curling crown.

Heartland

We yearn for the face
of the beloved, even
the pockmarked face:

skunk cabbage hollow in August
after the leaves dissolve
and contractile roots pull
the plant's core deeper into ooze—

the hollow's flood-smoothed
surfaces punctuated
by holes defining the plant
through negative space.

So we too are pocked,
marked by longing in any land
free from this familiar blemish.

An "imperfect idea"

       is how the Provincial Assembly in 1726 described native recollection
       of a writ from Penn re-granting Lenape ownership of land a mile to either
       side of the Brandywine. Yet the Lenape remembered it perfectly:

*Which writing was, by the burning of a cabin, destroyed; but we all remember very well
the contents thereof: That William Penn promised that we should not be molested*

*whilst one Indian lived, grew old, and blind and died,—so another, to the third
generation; and now it is not half the age of an old man since, and we are molested,*

*our lands surveyed out and settled before we can reap our corn off;
and to our great injury, Brandywine Creek is so obstructed with dams,*

*that the fish cannot come up to our habitations. We desire you to take notice
that we are a poor people, and want the benefit of the fish, for when we are out hunting,*

*our children with their bows and arrows, used to get fish for their sustenance…
we desire that those dams be removed, that the fish may have their natural course.'*

'How did you understand that writing to be?

       (asked the Assembly, obsessing over the missing writ,
       taking no apparent notice of starving children—)

That you should enjoy that land forever?'

*Not only we, but all the Indians understood it to be theirs
as long as the waters ran down the creek.*

       (What response could the Assembly make?
       Unsettled by the exchange, they bought time.)

'Have you anything more to say?'

No; but if you hear us not we shall be obliged to come again next spring.

       (Whereupon the Assembly, muttering among itself, called Nate
       Newlin, offering replacement lands in exchange for all rights
       to the Brandywine. Newlin took the offered lands, went on
       damming the creek, selling Lenape land with the corn
       still standing. The delegation came again as promised.

       Still the dams obstruct the fish. Still children go hungry.)

Amphibious

Turtle beds, I imagined, seeing turtles bask
on a sunny log, their shells the shell game
missing from the sand below.
                                           But no—
a friend, mother of a budding fisherman,
taught me to see instead the fish sweeping
debris from the creek bed: male fish, sculpting
with their tails these ovals a little longer
than their bodies, building stony nests
to woo a mate, to host a swarm of eggs.

Once you know to look, you can't help but see
that whole line of nests, down where the creek
curves south and the shallows catch full sun.
For years I passed, unseeing, as those fish
nests sketched an amphibious world,
modeled the same rules in force above and below
the water's blazing, blinding surface—

a world where today we might see sunfish
sail through the clouds, or tomorrow discover
a swallow of bluegills nesting on the river's bed.
Hear them sing of summer in a different key,
as we startle, our constellated bodies
recreating their watery swirl.

Mycorrhizae

If we were fungi, maybe
        we would send our hearts
                like digestive enzymes
        out into our surroundings,

curiosity & wonder turning us
        inside out, making
                rainbows from rigidity:
        blue-green cups,

neon-orange chicken
        of the woods, white
                oysters gathering
        strands of cellulose,

ascomycetes delivering
        a blue stain prized
                by woodworkers.
        If our words could succor

us into soil, would we play a part
        in this strange alchemy?
                Or would we still stumble
        over language like a fallen log,

where brown rot colors
        the wood a rich red,
                cellulose consumed,
        lignins left behind,

crackling into cubes
        that will one day crumble
                into particles full of mystery
        and life-giving water?

II. Surfacing

Snow-melt carrion call

Bloom after uncanny bloom punctuates
the crust of old snow like a pastry chef's stylish swirl,
or an unlikely upside-down exclamation point,

always ready to droop over its own opening;
or like a purpling-green bruise to mark the aftermath
of a blow, flesh thick and marred, mottled by its unlikely rise.

Come into my sauna, said the cabbage to the fly:
what other plant can melt the snow, bring the heat of sultry
summer? Where the spathe is scored or damaged, the light

shines cranberry red, neon pink, pulsing to the eye's darkening sight.
Stone flies, blow flies, scavengers, bees—February's fit audience
though few—*Symplocarpus* performs for them, not you:

its spathe a sheath, barely exposing the spadix within,
the spadix that elongated globe, sessile flowers rising like the spikes
of a novel virus from its moon-white, strobe-light dance floor.

Sycamore shelter
the Pringle Tree, 1764-67

                    Two brothers, deserters
                    from the king's army, flee
                    into wilderness. Near Turkey Run,
         they shelter   in a hollow
         sycamore until   their ammo
         runs out. John leaves   Samuel eking out
         his last two shots   (deer: missed; buffalo:
         hit), aiming for news   and provisions
                                         from a trading post
         on Shenandoah.   War's end frees
         them to gather more   settlers and return.
         Some say Samuel   brings his bride to share
         the sycamore: settlers, a breeding pair.
                    South from   today's Pittsburgh, west
         from Washington DC,   the Pringle tree
         has died twice above   ground—once by disease,
         once by flood—   but still it stands, its own
         third generation, re-   growing from life
         persistent in the root,   only to find
         itself fenced in,   constraint commemorating—
             what exactly?   its own survival?
             military desert   ers? settlers?
             human fort   itude or folly?

And why do we celebrate size,   resurrection, longevity
    in the very species we split   and grind to tiny fragments?

Cicada courtship

To strengthen
  their courting songs,
    these males hollow
      themselves till light
        almost shines
          through, making
            a resonating
            chamber
              of their abdomens,
            shoving
            essential organs
          aside, since
          there's nothing
        more essential
      than courtship:
    raw need
    amplified
by emptiness.

All day, late summer into fall, female cicadas are listening as males muscle
their abdominal instruments, their timbals, squeezing their struts
so they buckle and pop in one fast trill, then cascade back. Periodic cicadas wait
thirteen or seventeen years for this brief season above ground; even
the annual species have dug and chambered, tunneled through the earth
for years. Does emergence feel like looming death or transfiguration? or both?

Badda boom,
  badda bang,
    lockin and poppin,
      they're all percussion,
        all pulsating buzz:
          the lyric cicada's
            rattling trill;
              scissor-grinder cicadas,
                pulsing on a rising
                note, like a game of crack
            the whip that sends
            the sound flying; this blue-
          green cicada oscillating
        like a saltshaker, a staccato
      shimmy; the swamp
    cicada's fast crescendo,
  aggressive as a machine
gun's rat-a-tat.

Gunpowder, 1776

Well, who'd have thought that niter would be so hard to make, with Philly near, all full of piss & promise? The war council, calling itself a committee of safety, invited proposals for powder mills, & Robert Harris, physician sworn to protect human health, took the committee's cash, promised to repay in tons of gunpowder, built a mill on Crum creek, up & running in four months.

The recipe:
        100 parts saltpeter
        18 parts charcoal
        15 parts sulphur (also called brimstone).
For charcoal:
        season local dogwood,
        dig a pit, pile the wood,
        cover with straw and sod,
        set it on fire through a central chimney.
        Two years to season,
        a day to build the pit,
        a day to carbonize,
        two days to extinguish & cool the coal.
For brimstone:
        break up fool's gold,
        heat it to produce fumes
        that solidify as sulphur.
For saltpeter:
        pour urine over compost soils;
        wait, then harvest crystals of potassium nitrate—
                which wouldn't grow, or not reliably, not even after they hired
                a specialist from York, Pa, to teach them how it was done.
                Easier to import, despite the British ban.

Other gunpowder mills exploded; this one fizzled. Within a year, the mill had closed, cash repaid in tons of powder, leaving this residue:

        Brimstone from fool's gold.
        Charcoal's strangled fire.
        Saltpetre's pissy sublimations.

                That gunpowder mill.
                That revolution:
                      teaching us to live
                      on edge,
                      ammo at the ready.

Fiddlehead tonic

North: fiddleheads are called mahsus,
translated, maybe badly, as good magic.
My tongue stumbles on unfamiliar word-shapes:

the river Wolastoq, inhabited
by the Wolastoqiyik, people
of the beautiful river, who feed mahsus

to starving refugees, loyalists fleeing
the British defeat. The Wolastoqiyik
eat the vitamin-rich spirals as spring tonic,

some cooking the whole crown on heated stones
beneath spreading branches. The refugee-colonists
take the tonic, the good magic, very much to heart:

> *Fiddleheads steamed or boiled with butter and lemon,*
> *or pickled in vinegar three ways: try pepper,*

> *nutmeg, cinnamon, allspice; or garlic and dill;*
> *or onions, sugar, turmeric, mustard seeds.*

> *Steam or boil, roast or grill, mix with buttermilk,*
> *cornstarch, dijon mustard, tarragon, lemon juice.*

I have no heated stones, no spread branches,
but between my teeth, the earthy crunch of spring,
good magic hiding under far-fetched seasonings.

Nettled

Damp river bottom, late spring, one watershed west:
I labor to dig out entrenched and noxious weeds,
mostly multiflora rose. Nettle is welcome

to remain, but it does not welcome me.
Stung so often, my body shifts from sting

or burn to paresthesia: now arms and legs
buzz and fizz, reminding me of giving birth,
wired up to a device designed to ease

contractions—electrodes dialing up the buzz
as the pain grows, swells, crests, and opens.

What do nettles birth in us, despite ourselves,
the histamine rash manifesting
our familiar state: rankled, ruffled, riled?

What's in this prick of a plant, leaves and stalks
stocked with miniature sharp-edged hypodermics?

Silicon syringes full of histamine,
serotonin, acetylcholine—
a pharmacy full of drugs that don't quite explain

the sharpness of the nettle's sting,
nor the path by which the bite eases

aching muscles, aging joints—or the reason
why nettle packs these neurotransmitters,
bringing chemical guns to a knife fight

with a species so easily galled, piqued, provoked.
Can you exploit the homeopathy of pain,

trade arthritis for urtication?
Or is flogging with nettles just what it seems:
a punishing plant-based torment whose sting

and burn and bite linger as it leaves
no lasting mark, dissolving back to air?

Ghost bowing

Romy, my sister's child, fiddlehead
of the best kind, bends over the scroll
of their fiddle, its spiral dancing as the bow leaps
up; improvised ornaments, ghost-
bowing syncopation, and double-stopped drone
as percussive as their fast feet lightly stomping,
heel-and-toe, close to the floor, bowhairs snapping
in the dim cottage light.

                           Tragedy toils
behind the good magic of their playing:
near Wolastoq, the beautiful river, displaced
people battle to displace other settlers both
old and new. Romy's ghostly syncopations
recall the rhythms of French Acadia, people sharing
words, foods, raids with Mi'kmaw hosts, but refusing
oaths of loyalty to the conquering British.
Exiled from their non-native land, many
perish at sea in enemy ships.
The grand dérangement.

                         New settlers dispute
Mi'kmaw sovereignty for centuries. The Scots who take
the land carry their own displaced histories:
clansmen slaughtered in the Highland clearances;
evicted families emigrating to a world new
to them, bringing their reels, their music, rebellions
replayed in the stepping feet, counterpoint
to Acadian ghost-bowings.

                         Drums and dancers,
fiddleheads consoling the forlorn: all still here
for those still listening, like the Wolastoqiyik drums—
still playing, still improvising, still here,
even as Mi'kmaw fishing lines are cut,
boats burned, a warehouse incinerated; food supplies
further ghosted by wildfire and ocean heatwave.

Grasped
> *Whatever you do, do with all your might.*

They blame it on Aesop, that patriarchal tale:
small boy, nettled, runs crying to mom or dad,
is told to man up in no uncertain terms.

Clearly not a connoisseur of nettles,
that imaginary Aesop, scolding small boys:
"Touch something gently, and you'll be stung; seize it
boldly, gripe it fast, and it will never sting you."
"Many sorts of persons, as well as things,
ought to be treated in the same manner,"
adds the Victorian version.
                                        In pegging
the moral to Aesop, perhaps the patriarchs
meant to evoke the freed slave heading to Delphi,
a diplomat for Croesus, that king whose name
became a byword for wealth—but did they remember
that Aesop offended his prickly hosts
by telling fables they found insulting, until they
trumped up a charge of temple theft and chucked
him off a cliff? What's the moral there?

While the boy cries, perhaps his sister sits
in the meadow, considers the nettle,
follows the angle of the spikes up from the ground,
wraps hand in skirt, presses the spikes softly down
to avoid the sting while picking the greens
for nettle soup.
                                When her brother comes
crying back, to test his mettle, grasp it fast,
does she slow him, show him a gentler feast?

The rapture

With raptors on all sides, how did humans come
to imagine rapture as sanctuary? Even in Bible

verses, being rapt—*harpazo*—means to be snatched,
seized, caught up: terror, even in the hands of God.

Last month, a sharp-shinned hawk swooped past me, diving
through a neighbor's rhododendrons to grasp

a jeering blue jay out of its illusions
of safety on a leafy branch. The jay's weight

slowed the hawk's rise, twisting its trajectory,
swinging it close to my own steps, its wingtips

inches from my eyes, prey dangling from lowered legs
as those wings scooped air, laboriously climbing.

Last week, a Cooper's hawk rifled the broad branches
of my neighbor's dogwood, summoned by the rustle

of robins feasting on dogwood drupes, themselves turned feast.
Today: a red-shouldered hawk lands on the corner

of my deck, stares at me through kitchen windows,
trapping me in a gaze that shapes its own piercing

plunging dive. I strain to take in the pale grey
head, implacable; the long white chest speckled

with brown, breast slightly puffed, drawn up, as it pauses,
perches, eyeing the chipmunk in its tomato-pot

    sanctuary.   Blink and the raptor's gone.

Buttonwood agreement, 1792

Behind the agreement, a panic: a trader
over-leveraged, too big to fail, bailed out
by Alex Hamilton and the First Bank.

The result: a founding myth of the New
York Stock Exchange. Twenty-four men sign
a document of two sentences, named

for the sycamore where they used to meet
before their coffeehouse trading. The agreement:
to trade only with each other, for fixed

commissions, no under-cutting prices.
This private club, this gentlemen's agreement,
persists until Mayday 1975

when the SEC breaks the monopoly.
Can you imagine the breezy intimacy
of those early meetings, just four blocks

from the river and port, two and a half
blocks from the municipal slave market,
closed some thirty years before?

Enslaved people helped build the wall that gave
the street its name. Perhaps the sycamore,
the buttonwood, seemed an apt mascot

for a financial system the traders hoped would be
fast-growing, immense, durable, its roots
extending invisibly underground,

its young leaves covered with tiny hairs, revealed
under magnification as stars. But who
did the agreement, like the sycamore, sustain?

Years later, Audubon, himself a trader
in human flesh, would see thousands of finches
pouring in and out of a hollow sycamore.

The tree with its starry five-fingered leaves
vanished from Wall Street long ago; now only skyscrapers
and bankers cast shade, extend the reach of myth,

obscure the panic, the marketing
of human beings, shadow the agreement's
outer bounds until we barely remember

the place of the buttonwood, its finches,
its seed balls, its coarse-grained wood able to withstand
fine milling without cracks, its promise of relief.

Metamorphosis

Water strider instars flee and forage,
leaping free of attacking beak and wing,
eating enough to grow and force,
force their bodies through five separate molts,
emerging again and again through a y-shaped crack
at the back of head and thorax.

They dine on dragons four times their size,
on terrestrial insects gone astray,
on mosquito wrigglers and tumblers—
squirmy sperm-like larvae, and comma-shaped pupae,
both hanging from the water's surface, bugs
breathing through abdominal snorkel-like tubes—

or on this bee, this particular bee, who bumbled
onto the water and can't break free. The vibrations
from its thrashing call the strider who punctures its prey,
injects it with enzymes to liquidate the organs
it then sucks out through the same hollow straw: dark
metamorphosis feeding the strider's own transfigurations.

Retted

An old story: six brothers, one sister;
their kingly father gets lost in the woods,
agrees, unwise, to an uneasy marriage,
then hides the kids. New stepmom finds

them, sews magic shirts, turns the boys to swans.
The sister, abandoned to human loneliness,
has to save the day with shirts of nettle
shaped through six years' silence to change

them back. I always imagined the nettles stinging
throughout those years of labor, the girl's
pain required to unmake the false mother's
shaping and bring the brothers home. But no:

weaving with nettles demands not pain
but time: months for the nettles to grow tall,
a week or more to soak the stalks, dissolve
the sting, extract the core, scrape off all

woody parts, leaving only bast fibers
to spin and weave and sew, creating
tensile strength, unlimited flexibility.
Not the nettles but the passing years inflict pain:

forced silence like a burnt lip, stung tongue.
The brothers lose her after a neighbor-king
tracks her to her hut. Without brothers or voice,
cornered but steadfast, she is wed silently,

copes with the marriage bed in silence; bears
children through the pains of childbirth, silence
her only recourse, till, slandered by court intrigue,
her silence is no defense. What does it mean to choose

lost brothers over unwilled offspring? Imprisoned,
condemned to death, she hoards her silence, weaving.
Approaching the stake, arms full of nettle cloth, she
herself is all bast fibre, all tensile strength,

flexed to retrieve those brothers, who still seek her
amid their own twice daily transformations,
swan to boy to swan. Do they fight the change,
fight to keep the hot blood of their swan nature,

its strong stroking flight, quick breath and sharp vision,
more comforting, more familiar now than boyhood?
When they arrive to save her from the stake,
do they see their sister-swan in her humanity,

bones hollowed out by suffering, her song
so long silenced by the rules that caged her?
Are they freed or nettled by the work
of her hands? Do they feel, as she does,

the unspoken suffering unspooling fast,
watching time slide through those unfeathering
fingers? Nettle shirts once on, are they—
any of them—ever free of the weave?

Plush

As the settlers shift from sustenance to surplus,
their mills make not just artifacts but tenements
and workers. The plush mill upstream weaves worsted
fabric on a metal frame: when the work is done,

a knife slides between the layers and slices,
creating one face of fabric above
and one below, all the hairs standing stiff on end—
for a while, the very definition of luxury.

The ramshackle buildings of the gunpowder mill
are shaping and sharpening scythes by '26,
the whine and screech of metal against stone
competing with the deeper roar of water over the dam;

by '30, the mill is making paper,
likely from linen, hemp, cotton fragments;
fifteen years later, the creek's force turns
spinning jennies, power looms to make the cotton

the earlier mill once shredded. Stale urine
used to felt fabric at the fuller's mill
can be smelled a mile off, even near the Leiper
mill turning tobacco to snuff for the man's land-

speculator friends, Washington and Jefferson.
By mid-century the land is lousy with mills,
this one driving a forge, that one cutting
logs to planks, the next grinding flour. Economies

built on scale and convenience split the faces
of workers from those of owners with a knife's
edge sharpened by rheumatoid arthritis, by tumors,
by renal failure from the inflammation

with which the body responds to flour dust,
cotton dust, sawdust, long hours, submission
to a structure not designed to sustain
the people who every day go through the mill.

Bedrock

shapes topography,
the ground of possibility.

Crooked creek cuts
through soft schist,
turns at hard gneiss,
carving gorges below
what was once the level
of the forest floor.

Without the creek, no gorge;
without the gorge, no woods.

Farmers clearcut the land,
but stopped where slopes grew
too steep to farm.
The land's refusal. Refuge.

Volunteers
    winter 1892

Their gazes pierce the flat photograph's greyscale calm.
Poised, full of implied motion even in the frozen
moment, they could be about to smile, or complain at the forced

stillness, or finish a joke told under the breath. Is the snow melting
through their clothes? You wouldn't know: they seem at ease,
sitting, kneeling, framed by the patchy white snow of the hillside.

A sports team, the librarian tells me, in team uniforms, except
for the man in back with cane and bowler hat, perhaps the manager.
The still image captures the uniforms' pinch and pull, the shirts

cross-laced up the center line of the owners' torsos. One bears
the numbers 92; another, 94. I imagine the numbers as class years
until I remember that the college won't accept Black students

for another half century. I am in the Friends' Historical Library, researching
the woods, which of course are never distant from the pinch and pull
of human life. I have to keep correcting my assumptions: forty years before

the Civilian Conservation Corps. Before the Great Migration. These men
likely built the Historically Black neighborhood of Swarthmore from scratch, sent
their children to the segregated school, now dismantled, whose curb-cut

is still visible half a block from the house where I live. Their caps stake out
different personalities: striped or solid, worn forward, backward, visor
up or down, a beret at the back, a stocking cap with a large pompom, partly

obscured by the sign the man holds: Volunteers. What did they volunteer
to do? Who needed to know? And what of the white girl behind the lens?
A student wealthy enough to own a personal camera when even the college

yearbook had only a handful of photos. A few of her photos appear in the year
book for 1892, but her personal album overflows. Skilled with tripod, focus
and settings, stubborn enough to carry the bulky machine into the woods,

perhaps with help. This photo of volunteers wasn't taken in passing. Who made
the arrangements? Who lettered the sign? I page through the album, looking
for context: landscapes, interiors, several sporting events, none with Black

athletes. At the turn of the century, the College rejected an accepted student
once they realized he was Black. In 1933, another rejection: the College President
wrote to the editor of Baltimore's *Afro-American* to explain *the life here is very intimate*

so it would be hard to make a Negro student comfortable because (note the repetition and variation) the College was run on *such intimate coeducational lines*. The fear of miscegenation not far below the surface. Students protested, to no avail. First

accepted Black students, 1943: two women. Back in 1892, the photographer blew up a detail from the group of volunteers, focusing on the man in the striped jersey. He holds a ball; a faded serpentine S cuts across the stripes of his shirt. Elsewhere,

two white male musicians in formal dress are likewise doubled out of a group portrait, given their own page, presumably a sign of their importance to the photographer. But only this Black man in the striped jersey appears three times,

the third time a full-length portrait: he stands in front of a tree, amid dry ferns, left leg crossed over right, left hand in pocket. Now he wears high-waisted, discreetly checked trousers, high-collared shirt and light tie, a waistcoat and jacket with velvety collar.

I can't read his gaze. What does he see in her or she in him? Is this a portrait of desire? Respect? What did they volunteer for, alone or together? And what business is it of mine, more than a century later—except to wonder what exercise of will

is called for now, what forms of respect and intimacy might start to repair long centuries of damage. Photos of undergrads piling snowballs on their heads, smoking cheroots barefoot in the creek, seem stuck in a past deceptively free

of care, but the faces of these volunteers still speak to the present. What do we have the skill and the will to heal? What ground do we stand on? What relations do we acknowledge? I recognize that frozen hillside. Weathered grit spills

from the cracked stone behind the volunteers; a thin trickle of snowmelt, refrozen, serpentines above that sediment, like an S with the leading edge disappearing behind the lip of the boulder, that hard gneiss formation.

Reading the forested landscape

Rock weathers into soil
at the ridgeline,
rain etching with acid
while lichen crusts, fingers,
lifts the surface from the stone.

Ferns suture the wounded hillside,
holding back erosion;
mosses bloom valedictory
on the trail's edge,
red stalks rising from green carpet.

Ten years ago, that stone
bench halfway up the bare
hillside was hidden
behind green understory.
Deer browse: deadly.

You've lost the plot,
my sister says. Don't you see
that every loss is opportunity,
every deficit a chance to start again?
No. Here is what I see:

stories stuttering through deficits,
lingering on loss: logging, storm, fire,
blight, invasion, extinction.
Have we nothing else to read?
no other tales to tell?

Beech

Imagine a beech not as a plant but as a world,
with forty birds and mammals crowding that towering world.

In old English *boc* meant both book and rooted beech:
between these covers, a not-yet-imagined world.

Moths, butterflies, weevils congregate on furrowed leaves,
roll themselves a shelter as if it were a world.

Underground, a fungus big as a blue whale:
a different Atlas reshouldering a weary world.

Woolly beech aphid waves its woolly butt at us:
a workshop of honeydew, sugaring the world.

A beech holds space and silence for hundreds of years;
imagine the secrets we'd whisper in such a world.

Epifagus flowers: an uncanny sugar thief,
tapping beech roots beneath our sun-blind world.

The twisted lines of a snapped beech demand new readings
as the species spreads in this warming, broken world.

Chickadees nesting in its cavities remind us:
a plant can be a planet, rebirthing the world.

Dredging

The dredgers' bare toes wriggle in the cool
shallows, below the summer morning's heat;
their calloused hands stick and slide on their shovels'

wooden handles, just as the silt sticks and slides
on the flat blades dipping in and out of the creek.
Mill-dams trap sediment, burying

rocky riverbeds, the spawning grounds
of native fish. Left alone, the dammed stream
will inundate the plain, make marshland. These boys

are dredging the creek to maintain mill flows.
For hundreds of years, as the water goes wide,
settlers dig deep. An eerie pas de deux:

species migrate through cloudy waters
to cooler climes, just as fish freshly adapted
to the newly shallow creek find their habitat

destroyed by dredging. And when the mills die back,
cities edge forward, cement the river banks,
sometimes bury the creeks all together.

The youngest dredger tosses a shovel-full
of silt at a nearby friend. His son will do
the same. His great-grandson, working at Boeing,

won't hear the splash, won't even know
the creek runs below. Our work now is daylighting:
reviving the ripples and pools of our past,
returning the creek to its place, us to ours.

III. Rapt

Surface tension

Water striders call to me, though I know
too well the brutal thrashing that dwells above
their dainty footprint: they live on power
and speed, poised on a vast vibrating medium,

a web of stories overheard, stories
submerged in one another, amplifying
or canceling each other out, stories
my dull ears can't discern, though I

dream of decoding the morse messages
of wave and ripple, meanings dancing
through the body, from the orgasmic
irregular intensity of a feast

wriggling on the water nearby
to the communal force of fellow instars
swarming the water's surface, like stars spangling
the stream, mirroring the night sky;

I imagine the lift-off from the surface,
the landing in which an embrace of air
keeps the water's surface ever dry;
in this paradox of liminal life,

I celebrate the sharpening edge.

Rapture: early lessons

Walking backward as instructed, facing
the silken sail, keeping it steady,
I am baffled to hear the instructor

saying my name, telling me not to panic.
I am learning to paraglide: a windy day,
an early lesson, working in a dip

of the hill to stay grounded. Glancing back
at the teacher, I find myself thirty feet above
ground. Rapt. The difference between land and sky

shockingly imperceptible, like a quiet
version of the whirlwind snatching Elijah,
or Paul's third heaven, *whether in the body*

or out of the body I do not know, God knows.
Is that rapture? Miracles made quotidian,
unmiraculous? The week before, I had seen

a man plummet like Icarus to earth, had raced,
panicky, across the pasture toward him
and his triply broken leg, amazed by his stoic

self-possession amid pain and fear. *Don't look
at the brambles*, the teacher says, coaxing me
to turn and face forward, to seek a stairway

back from the clouds. *Body follows vision. Don't look
where you don't want to go.* But I am helpless, rapt,
the thorns snatching me home as I stumble from the sky.

Tunnel dreams

1.

Claustrophobic, trapped in nightmare,
I am worming my way through enclosing earth:
heavy, damp, dark. My breath echoes

back from stony soil inches away, misting
my face, clogging my throat as muscles scream
in exhaustion. Sluggish in my waking,

I recognize the story my dream replayed,
one my sister had re-told the night before, a tale
of redemption my mother had loved and repeated:

an arrogant neuroscientist dies, then returns
with tales of the afterlife, of his long labor
through the dirt to bright lights, explosive love.

By dawn my sister has gone to join
our brothers at our mother's bedside;
they will call if there is any change.

I take hours to catch my breath, check my work—
they will call if there is any change—
but no one calls and when I drag myself

to the nursing home I hear the death rattle
from the doorway and I feel in my bones
that the dream that woke me was my mother's journey.

2.

Before her words wandered out of reach, my mother
described her own death as a train voyage:
people will get off at different stops, while I

go on. The nursing-home room is crowded
with her children and step-children; none of us
skilled at saying goodbye. Too late to learn? My

sister-in-law delivers an Anglican prayer;
I sing quietly, voice low so no one will make
me stop. As the morning wears on, we start

to wonder how far we can bear to go, flayed
by our mother's rasping breath, each inhalation
like a burrowing through stony air—or, as fluid

fills the lungs, a gurgling through rising water.
As my stepbrother stands to leave, I remind
our mother, *sotto voce*, of the scientist

struggling wormlike through the earth, to burst
into light: *You're almost there. Almost—*
The impasse and the moment break with shocking

speed. Eyes and brow flick up, her torso yearns skyward:
Bye—the word part exhalation, part farewell—
and then she's gone, the ties that held her snapped,

leaving in this heavy soil the vibration
of her passing, the light burrowing down
to linger in our late-waking hearts.

Spiral

The fiddlehead fern predates the fiddle,
follows a different curve—the slow growth
of a ram's horns or a nautilus' chambers,
the outward turn of a savanna elephant's
tusks, the quickening trajectory of moth
to flame or peregrine falcon attacking its prey.

Spira mirabilis, the wonderful spiral:
proportional, equiangular,
for Jacob Bernoulli a symbol
"either of fortitude or of constancy
in adversity, or of the human body…
restored to its exact and perfect self."
On his grave: *eadem mutate resurgo.*
though changed, I rise again the same.

Writing

When the children bring buckets of worms
from the nearby woods to the kindergarten door,
the teachers tell them they can spell
out their words in twists and twirls: the worm
flesh threshing at the salt on human hands,
alphabets squirming. An *A*-line, unmoored,
becomes a cursive *Z*, an *I* serpentining
as the worms head writhing for the woods.

Some of us never grow beyond our childhood loves,
the sting of our salt hands on the beloved
unnoticed, unregarded, while connections slither
away like worms floundering across our barren
understanding, leaving these fertile castings we
manhandle: our loving still too fierce, too fond.

Impounded, 1931

I know how to rescue a dog from the pound,
a car from the impoundment lot, but not a creek
from a reservoir. History brings us here, but no

farther: by 1880, water mills give way
to steam boilers, mill buildings abandoned
or repurposed. Now railroads cross the creeks, bringing

elites to new suburban estates, green dreams carved
from farms parceled out to highest bidders.
An engineering professor joins a land company,

helps build a stone tower to distribute water
to the housing tracts. The College burns, rebuilds,
uses the old mill to drive a water system

moving fifty thousand gallons a day.
Shovel-ready at the start of the Great
Depression, the Springton Reservoir,

impounding four billion gallons, rises
to meet suburban Philadelphia's future
demands. Impound: 1. To seize and take

legal custody due to an infringed
law or regulation. 2. To shut up
domestic animals. 3. To hold back

or confine water. What laws did the creek
infringe? Can water be domesticated?
By 1931, earthen embankments rip-rapped

with rock fill confine Crum Creek. A highway runs
across the dam, a sign proclaiming the water
thus impounded private property.

Water companies spring up, merge, consume
one another up the corporate food chain.
The state leaves the creek in the custody

of corporations: a foster child, confined,
surveilled. Impounded. And none of us imagines
choosing differently, none of us

would build an outhouse in the back or carry
water from the creek for daily use.
Our histories of water, unconsidered;

our futures, still unconceived. We know
so little of ourselves and this wet land:
all of us surveilled, confined, all

foster children of the mills that made us.

Discernment

Water striders grow large wings, small wings,
no wings at all—broad wings to leave a vanishing

habitat, small or none to avoid a capsize
in rough water, or to speed ever faster

on the surface in a calm, stable home.
Some say water strider parents choose: this

generation needs strength, this one needs flight.
And how will humans choose: how will we shape

our descendants, buffeted in rough
and vanishing homelands? I choose flight, I choose

it not. Child, take this thimbleful of speed
to keep you nimble in the face of leaping

death. I see you, child, with your translucent wings
of hard-won wisdom: be prepared to set

them down before the waves whip high. Children,
may you discern what we did not: what the world

asks of you, how it sings to you, how threat
can still be promise, perhaps a guide, whisper-light.

Jewelweed

1.
Liminal spirits of the creekside build
hollow stalks, translucent when backlit, with leaves
that shun water, hold it at arm's length,
shaping droplets to lift contamination

and dust from surfaces that spin sunshine to sugar.
Their blossoms—yellow or speckled orange—
dangle like fleshy earrings between layers
of jewel-laden leaves, their tunneled spurs

a lure to the bumble bee's long and supple tongue,
offering nectar for the plump body
spreading pollen dust across clumping communities.

Every year impatiens takes its time,
devotes every moment of sweet life
to the shaping of something just out of reach.

2.
Within maturing pods, columella
cradles seeds as five outer valves prepare
to fire: stronger than steel springs,

made taut with root-drawn water,
the valve's coils curve, strain, ready
for release. A brush, a squeeze:

a mature pod explodes, launching the seeds.
Sometimes the coiled valves, curled in tiny rings,
fall, still taut, into your fraught, startled palm.

Imagine labor at your fingertips,
seedpods exploding from each extremity,
your body still choosing, launch after launch,

to cast its treasures onto wind and soil
and the water that carries new life to new lands.

Natural history

These years of beauty are also years of damage:
Baldwin locomotive, Boeing aircraft
cover the mouth of the Crum, gag the creek
with cement, heavy machinery, forgings,
tool steel, ship propellers, heavy castings, mining.
Decades now and still no idea
of thinking like a creek: the sand washes
downstream from the water treatment plant
no one can visit, not since 9/11.
Sewer lines, pipelines, train trestles criss-cross
the creek's length; shredders gorge on clear-cut trees;
explosives consume the hogback knoll that once ruled
the waters of the valley—till beavers return
to re-shape a landscape both familiar and forgotten.

Repair

                                        A man in a cab
                                    caterpillar-treading
                                      along the creek,
                                     extends his boom,
                                    his slowmo explosion
                                      of spinning blades,

                            and the mulching head

                              bites the sycamore's

                            broad, devalued trunk,

                                spewing fragments,

                            unbuttoning   wood

                         into   spring   air:

                    sycamores   roto-rooted   above ground

        to   re-clear   the   suburbs'

            ancient   sewer   line.

Worm sex

The only time I ever watched, voyeur,
the act in progress, was on the playing field
where we ran the dogs in the morning:
misty rain that day and muddy ground
and there they stretched, inverted U's, clasping
each other by the clitellum, glued
to one another with a slime tube
swathing their conjoined, conjugal bodies.

I gaped at their unexpected length,
and the speed with which they sprang apart,
diving into their burrows with the snap
of a rubber or a rubber band
breaking or loosed; *coitus interruptus*
for a species used to *prolongatus*:
known to spend three hours or more in that clinch,
hermaphroditic, a joint ejaculation

carried through slime to sperm receptacle.
Back home, I discovered that despite the courtship,
that extended clasp, worm reproduction
is lonely, solitary, a slime tube
like a sweater pulled over the head
scooping up eggs, then sperm, enclosing all
in a lemon-shaped cocoon, with albumin
to feed the worms-to-be. On this field of queer sex,

I wanted to celebrate how each worm inhabits
all positions of erotic exchange,
but found myself distracted by worm housekeeping:
that tidy morphing of bodily fluids
into a package made to keep the kids
fed and happy, self-sufficient, their parents
free to lose themselves, after their courtship
and its consummation, in consuming the earth.

It looks like rage

rules water strider sex: males gripe,
grab, grapple; females fight, flee, evolve
genital shields—only to find
their evolutionary triumph unraveled:
males climb onto females' back to drum

rhythms on the water, summoning
predators—a pattern they cease only when
the female submits, lowers her shield,
permits penetration.

                        Some females make
the best of a bad bargain, allow
post-coital guarding, the male riding them,
draining their energy but fending off
the next attack.   Others refuse.

                                Harassed,
females seek refuge away from water,
foraging, and food, reducing mating
opportunities for all: hyper-aggression
favors the bully, harms the group.

Could be worse: male bedbugs stab females
through their abdominal walls, infecting
and inseminating with a single blow;
male cowpea seed beetles attack their mates
with a spiked penis that scars the vaginal tract.

Could be better: male nursery web spiders
present their mates with a silk-wrapped meal.
Male springtails drop spermatophores on the ground,
dancing to draw female attention. The sperm

packet of the rattlebox moth provides
life-long protection from predatory spiders.
Dancing flies sometimes offer art: a leaf, stone,
a silk balloon.

                    O dancing fly, bring me
your promise of persistence; your silk,
ballooning in the creek's soft breath,
your leaf, lifted by the wind.

Sanctuary

For most of us, a speck in the sky
is whatever the experts say it is.

We strive to see through their eyes, partitioning
the landscape. *Look two glasses above the slope*

of Pinnacle, they say. Now high over Owl's Head.
We are here for hawk migration, and the hawks

are here, too, evidently, but so high
above they barely register: kettles

of broad-wings circle, climbing thermals in groups
of twenty, forty, sixty, sometimes thousands.

I strive to care about something so distant,
out of sight. Distracted, I am thinking instead

about the people laboring up
the short climb to this summit, their unsteady

steps, fatigue, breathlessness, marking
what they treasure here: the old remembering

past summits, the young storing up
stories of wilderness. Turkey vultures circle close,

tipping side to side, their wings in that classic V.
Hunters on this Kittatiny ridge once shotgunned

thousands of migrating hawks each year until, appalled
by photos of the raptors' corpses arranged

in tidy rows, a New York socialite bought
the mountain to block the massacre.

From slaughter to sanctuary: what would
it take to make space for migrants

abandoned in the deserts, perishing
on open seas, water-cannoned, bloodied, caged?

An older man with good binoculars calls out:
Bald eagle on the left, beside the cell tower,

below the windmill ridge, the shuttered coal plant.
At the same time, an expert points high overhead:

we strain to see past our works and desolations
to the opening hidden in that dark cloud, that patch of blue.

Heartwood

What animal fouls its own home, its own
water, runs a sewer through a river
rather than under a road? We denature ourselves.

      Sometimes my mind feels   like the too-close walls
   of even a giant   sycamore,
    dark & dense   like the Pringle brothers',
     homestead   marked
by missing heartwood,   the ragged walls full
   of fluid rising   & falling like sap.

No fossils here

says the geologist: the pressure and heat
of continents colliding would have
obliterated any physical residue of life:

imagine a time-lapse of billions of years,
continents swirling across the surface
of this small planet, the mash-up

of continents thrusting mountains
two miles high into the sky. Right where
you stand, you'd be two miles deep

inside a mountain. But then erosion
grinds the mountains down as the supercontinent
slowly unravels, tectonic plates inching

across the globe. Subduction zones open.
Volcanic islands form off the coast,
come smashing in when Pangaea forms, sediment

metamorphosing into schist. Where the surface
cracks, magma wells up, metamorphoses
into banded gneiss, plates of schist, a few garnets.

How can we imagine life surviving
such crushing force? how envision life so
at odds with creek mud, dappled light, warm breath?

Insiders

Shorting the future, we mistake our position:
trading at the margins, on borrowed time,
lacking the material knowledge we need
to acquire more than the illusion

of our securities. Meanwhile, sycamores, a safe
distance from the sewer, stand sentinel
over the woods, sequestering carbon
by spinning wood from air, partnering

with red maple, black willow, to stabilize the banks
of the river. Six hundred years standing:
they've seen humans, wolves, bears killed and displaced,
communities unravelling amid a rash

of construction, workers singing, cursing,
as the growing village consumes the woods,
crudely exchanging a complex living
infrastructure for roads and dams and sewers.

Dark pools of liquidity replace
the vernal pools in which the future
swims toward the present. Our marginal existence
shifts under foot, under root. We look away.

Living fossils

"I spoke loosely," the biologist says,
"what I meant was not a taxon stranded
 in some back eddy of evolution,

but something more like a ghost twin, lost
in the womb, forlorn half of a missing whole.
Honey locust's spiky thorns do little

against deer scrape, deer browse: instead, they sketch
the long-lost woolly mammoth, its tusked mouth reaching
for the locust's sweet honey-like pod.

Forget recent history, those settlers using
thorns as nails to build a dwelling
when metal was scarce. If not the mammoth,

then perhaps giant beavers, twelve feet high,
or the short-faced bear, largest mammal recorded here.
All gone: just the tree—and we—remain."

"But what does it mean?" I ask. As we sit
with the locust, phantoms crowd the negative space
around its evolutionary niche. I touch its long thorn.

"To our own taxonomic twins, what fruit do we offer?
What archaic code roots us here?" He shrugs.
"Ten thousand years: the locust remembers,

offers its honey pods, clings to its armor.
Amid such stony recollection, even human fossils
might rediscover our ancient ebb and flow."

Flood

The pandemic was washing over the land
& we zoomed along, some thirty or forty gathered
in the name of safety & adaptation, & suddenly
suddenly the thunder was deafening, the lightning
right beside me & business—

business paused as people vanished,
their zoom squares blinking out
& the lights flickering off & on, off & on,
the faces freezing & unfreezing
in the zoom squares that remained—
& the rain so heavy those virtual voices vanished

or maybe I hit mute to listen
to the percussive force & wonder
at the weight-lifting of the clouds,
wonder whether Noah today would build
his ark not of wood but bits & bytes,
noticing how ark rhymes with arc,
completes the circle, noticing how just

for a few moments, a diluvian
world surged against the margins
of our zoom delusions & confusions,
short-circuiting our frames, each clash
of thunder re-defining what counts as safety
in a crashing world, freezing
& unfreezing beneath the virtual.

Hours later, my daughter & I stood
sobered, staggered by the water's sweep
across the drowned meadow, five feet under;
we surprised the land beaver, hedgehog keeping
one weather eye on the flood as he ducked
into his hillside den; we imagined

the beavers less fortunate as river sand flooded
their lodges. Birds & trees seemed unperturbed,
despite the force of the waters: calm
amid destruction.
     My daughter took
my hand & we stood together, learning
to leave space
    for the unimaginable.

Listen

: tulip poplar branches creaking, squirrels sneaking
acorns underground till swamp oaks grow,

grasses sighing with the soft winds, distant thunder,
fox footfall after furtive cottontails pass by,

herons' wings beating the air at take-off,
fish nesting as beavers nibble and dam,

a song of shapeshifting, transformation
beyond the fixed forms we assume when crisis comes.

Listen, says the creek.

I am listening
through the thick milkweed fluff of my ignorance.

Listen, says the creek,

      & tell me what you hear.

Taste

At the tap, a bitterness the water companies can't
purify. These days I try not to filter it out,

work to taste what I'm drinking, that hint of mill
waste discharged for centuries, now settled

in the silt backing up from dams still blocking
the fish from their courses. Other pollutants, too:

not just forever chemicals, unknown toxins,
but trace elements of denial, disregard,

a willed unknowing. Now I look for the effects
of long-term inundation, try to recognize

how power moves beyond my channeling,
let my imagination test its banks,

decode the daily invitation I only
sporadically accept: to dredge the poison

from my own mottled history, reach for daylight,
buffered by the trees' dappled shade.

Broken

Note the beauty of broken things: how the tree's
skin splinters as it grows, sloughing off in plates,
leaving the sycamore's upper surface mottled,
bark flaked gray, brown, greenish-white.

Weather-softened seedballs—buttonballs—break
open for mud season, feeding birds, beavers,
residents and migrants alike. Still, change
is in the air—warming, drying, wetter than we've

known before—and forests themselves are moving,
broad-leaves shifting west, pine trees heading north:
even tree communities can break and part,
heading toward their ancient Cretacean homes.

What can we see of this future we're making,
the mottled beauty that comes with our breaking?

Flight

My highest
flight: tandem

paragliding with a young
guide keen to share

his love of wind and sky.
Together, we stepped off

the mountainside,
skimmed the trees, rode

up the slope to the ridge
on air currents deflected

from ground and trees. We
caught a thermal, circled

higher. The world dropped
away down the far side

of that ridge,
seeming to double

our speed. Heart rising,
stomach dropping

into the wind.
Terror entwined

with spasming
delight, disbelief

that the thinning
air could still support

us, twisting, on edge amid
the spinning clouds.

Notes

I. Contact

Damsel

For names and parts of a mill, see among other sources Brixton windmill https://www.brixtonwindmill.org/about/history/history-in-16-objects/damsel/ as well as "Milling terms" http://www.flitwickmill.co.uk/mill/milling-terms, and Theodore Hazen's "History of Flour Milling in Early America" https://www.angelfire.com/journal/millrestoration/history.html

Mouth Art of the Bald-faced Hornet

For a hilarious description of investigating bald-faced hornet nests back in 1929, see Phil Rau, "The Nesting Habits of the Bald-Faced Hornet," Vespa Maculata, *Annals of the Entomological Society of America*, 22: 4 (1929): 659–675. https://doi.org/10.1093/aesa/22.4.659

For details about nest construction, see W. V. Balduf, Observations on the White-Faced Wasp Dolichovespula Maculata (Linn) (Vespidae, Hymenoptera), Annals of the Entomological Society of America, 47:3 (1954): 445–458. https://doi.org/10.1093/aesa/47.3.445

Hoerenkill, 1631

For a brief history of Zwaanendael and Hoerenkill, near today's Cape Henlopen in Delaware, see Jean R. Soderlund, *Lenape Country: Delaware Valley Society Before William Penn* (2016), pp. 38-44.

Fiddlehead feint

For an accessible overview of fern anatomy, see https://nearbynature.fwni.org/2018/10/23/ferns-and-fiddleheads-background/

The first Crum mill, 1643

For background on early European settler populations and their reliance on Lenape hosts, see Jean R. Soderlund, *Lenape Country: Delaware Valley Society Before William Penn* (2016), especially pp. 16, 58-61. In 1654, Swedish engineer Peter Lindeström noted that the Swedes frequently ran short of food and relied on Lenape maize (Soderlund 16).

Emergence

This poem re-tells a small part of the Lenape creation story, as told by a Lenape man known as Jasper to Peter Sluyter and Jasper Danckaerts:

"This," he said, "is a tortoise, lying in the water around it," and he moved his hand round the figure continuing, "This was or is all water, and so at first was the world or the earth, when the tortoise gradually raised its round back up high, and the water ran off of it, and thus the earth became dry." He then took a little straw and placed it on end in the middle of the figure and proceeded, "The earth was now dry, and there grew a tree in the middle of the earth, and the root of this tree sent forth a sprout beside it, and there grew upon it a man, who was the first male. This man was then alone, and would have remained alone; but the tree bent over until its top touched the earth, and there shot therein another root, from which came forth another sprout, and there grew upon it the woman, and from these two are all men produced." Sluyter, Peter, and Danckaerts, Jasper. *Journal of a Voyage to New York and a Tour in Several of the American Colonies in 1679-80.* The Long Island Historical Society, 1867.

Caleb Pusey's gristmill arrives
For details about Pusey's early career, see J. William Frost, "Unlikely Controversialists: Caleb Pusey and George Keith" *Quaker History,* Volume 64, Number 1, Spring 1975, pp. 16-36. Published by Friends Historical Association https://doi.org/10.1353/qkh.1975.0002. For Pusey's later recollections of early provincial history, see Henry J. Cadbury, "Caleb Pusey's Account of Pennsylvania," *Quaker History*, Volume 64, Number 1, Spring 1975, pp. 37-57. https://doi.org/10.1353/qkh.1975.0004

The flouring of Lenapehoking
Farmers in the English colonial period and into the early nineteenth century were able to produce substantial surpluses for trade. Grains, vegetables, livestock, tobacco and other products were sold in Philadelphia, Chester and other nearby markets and exported to other colonies and even Europe. The phrase "agents of empire" comes from a quotation in Soderlund, p. 48.

Habitat
For an explanation of water striders' ability to move on water, see Gao, Xuefeng, and Lei Jiang. "Water-repellent legs of water striders." Nature 432.7013 (2004): 36-36.

Mychorrhizae
For accessible details of different kinds of wood rotting fungi, see https://www.concordmonitor.com/The-Outside-Story-~-Wood-Rot-Rainbow-43383248

"An imperfect idea"
Quotations (in italics and quotation marks) from Wilmer W. Thompson, *Chester County and Its People*. Pennsylvania State University: 1898, 117-129.

Invasion
For a summary of the impact of non-native earthworms relevant to Pennsylvania and parts north, see https://haltonmastergardeners.com/2020/02/08/yes-earthworms-are-an-invasive-species-in-eastern-north-america/.

II. Surfacing

Snow-melt carrion call
Cyanide-resistant cellular respiration—an anaerobic respiration pathway—allows skunk cabbage to create its own heat, which enables it to melt snow and ice in order to bloom in February.

Spathe: a fleshy leaf-like bract, surrounding the spadix (see below).
Symplocarpus foetidus: the Latin name for skunk cabbage.
Spadix: a fleshy stem with small flowers; sessile flowers: borne directly on the stem, with no stalk.

Sycamore shelter
For details on (and photographs of) the Pringle tree, see https://www.hackerscreek.org/page-1075180 and https://www.onlyinyourstate.com/west-virginia/pringle-tree-wv/.

Cicada courtship
Looming death: after living from two to seventeen years underground, cicadas die within five weeks of emergence. For descriptions and recordings of the songs of cicadas, katydids, crickets and grasshoppers, see the wonderful resources at http://songsofinsects.com/

Gunpowder, 1776
See David Salay, "The production of gunpowder in Pennsylvania during the American Revolution" (1975). Harris' mill is described in Pa. Arch., Series 1, IV, 761; and, Robert Harris to Committee of Safety, May 29, 1776, Stewart Collection.

Fiddlehead tonic
For colonial era consumption of fiddleheads, see Patrick von Aderkas, "Economic History of Ostrich Fern, *Matteuccia struthiopteris,* the Edible Fiddlehead." *Economic Botany.* 38:1 (Jan-Mar 1984) pp. 14-23. (For correction of Malicete to Wolastoqiyik, see https://www.thecanadianencyclopedia.ca/en/article/maliseet) Fiddlehead recipes: see https://extension.umaine.edu/publications/4198e/

Nettled
Paresthesia: a burning or prickling sensation. Extended exposure to nettles can produce paresthesia that lingers long after the rash subsides.

For an account of stinging nettle's spicules, or tiny barbs, see Cummings AJ, Olsen M. "Mechanism of action of stinging nettles." *Wilderness Environ Med.* 2011 Jun 22(2):136-9. doi: 10.1016/j.wem.2011.01.001. Epub 2011 Jan 6. PMID: 21396858.

For an account of the chemicals involved in nettle's sting, see Anderson BE, Miller CJ, Adams DR. "Stinging nettle dermatitis." *American Journal of Contact Dermatatits.* 2003 Mar;14(1):44-6. doi: 10.2310/6620.2003.38719. PMID: 14744424, and Oliver F, Amon EU, Breathnach A, Francis DM, Sarathchandra P, Black AK, Greaves MW. Contact urticaria due to the common stinging nettle (Urtica dioica)—histological, ultrastructural and pharmacological studies. *Clinical and Experimental Dermatology.* 1991 Jan;16(1):1-7. doi: 10.1111/j.1365-2230.1991.tb00282.x. PMID: 2025924.

For an overview of traditional and medicinal uses of stinging nettle, see https://www.mountsinai.org/health-library/herb/stinging-nettle

Ghost bowing
For an overview of the Cape Breton music Romy was playing see https://jsis.washington.

edu/canada/music-collection/cape-brenton-music/ (Cape Breton is a little northeast of New Brunswick, on the coast of Nova Scotia, so I take some liberties here.)
    For Acadian ghost-bowing and syncopation, see https://static1.squarespace.com/static/54ac7644e4b041b86b0bbb16/t/556f6250e4b0467afc68c184/1433363024348/Acadian+Fiddling+Traditions.pdf
    For a glimpse into Wolastoq traditional songs, updated by Jeremy Dutcher, see https://www.billboard.com/articles/news/8290094/jeremy-dutcher-wolastoqiyuk-lintuwakonaw

Buttonwood Agreement, 1792
For some of the history behind the Buttonwood Agreement, see https://time.com/4777959/buttonwood-agreement-stock-exchange/

Retted
For the sister weaving shirts of nettle, see "The Six Swans" in Jacob and Wilhelm Grimm, *Grimm's Household Tales*, trans. Mrs. A.W. Hunt. G. Bell and sons, 1884.

Plush
For "Workshop of the world" see https://philadelphiaencyclopedia.org/archive/workshop-of-the-world/; For records of mills, fires, explosions, see http://genealogytrails.com/penn/delaware/delhistjorv1p4.html
    See also: https://founders.archives.gov/documents/Jefferson/98-01-02-3530 http://hdl.library.upenn.edu/1017/d/pacscl/LCP_LCPLeiper

Volunteers
This ekphrastic poem describes photographs found in the 1895 Bertha Lippincott Album (PA 10/08) at the Friends Historical Library of Swarthmore College, particularly group portrait #A0007231.

Reading the forested landscape
Tom Wessel's *Reading the Forested Landscape of New England* suggests topography, climate, and history as three dominant factors producing or "writing" the forested landscape. Modes of history shaping the landscape are mostly catastrophic: logging, disease, storm, and so on.

Beech
The largest honey mushroom, *Armillaria ostoyea*, is now understood to weigh more than three blue whales. https://www.smithsonianmag.com/smart-news/mushroom-massive-three-blue-whales-180970549/

Dredging
"Keeping the [Strath Haven] lake dredged of silt accumulation was a major part of mill maintenance" (Delaware County Planning Department 2001), Roger Latham's *Conservation and Stewardship Guide* 2003.

III. Rapt

Rapture: early lessons
Paul's third heaven: 2 Corinthians 12:2-4.

Spiral
See https://hikersnotebook.blog/flora/ferns-fern-allies-and-mosses/fiddlehead-fern/

Impounded, 1931
See H.S.R. McCurdy, "The Springton Dam and Reservoir," *Journal (American Water Works Association)* 24.7 (1932): 995-1004.

Jewelweed
See Marika Hayashi, Kara L. Feilich, David J. Ellerby, "The mechanics of explosive seed dispersal in orange jewelweed *(Impatiens capensis),*" *Journal of Experimental Botany,* Volume 60, Issue 7, May 2009, Pages 2045-2053, https://doiorg.proxy.swarthmore.edu/10.1093/jxb/erp070

Worm sex
For a brief summary of earthworm reproduction, see https://www.earthwormsoc.org.uk/lifecycle.

It looks like rage
For females making "the best of a bad job" when it comes to sexual harassment, see Watson, Paul J., Robert R. Stallmann, and Goran Arnqvist. "Sexual conflict and the energetic costs of mating and mate choice in water striders." *The American Naturalist* 151.1 (1998): 46-58.

For an analysis of the community costs of hyperaggressive males, see Wey, Tina W., et al. "Personalities and presence of hyperaggressive males influence male mating exclusivity and effective mating in stream water striders." *Behavioral ecology and sociobiology* 69.1 (2015): 27-37.

For gruesome details on bedbug and cowpea seed beetle sex, see https://cnx.org/contents/Cp8sC4k_@5.1:G7v3GrxX@3/Violent-Mating-Traumatic-Insemination-in-Bed-Bugs-and-other-Cimicids and https://www.smithsonianmag.com/smart-news/why-seed-beetles-are-caught-sexual-arms-race-180963465/

For nuptial gifts, see https://www.cell.com/current-biology/pdf/S0960-9822(11)00604-X.pdf.

Sanctuary
The plural word for raptors is a "kettle"—a kettle of vultures, a kettle of broadwing hawks, etc. "Two glasses above Pinnacle"—"two glasses" means the height of a binocular lens against the sky, times two. Pinnacle and Owl's Head are the names of two peaks visible from Hawk Mountain Sanctuary.

Acknowledgments

I am grateful to the editors of the following journals in which poems previously appeared, sometimes with different titles or in slightly different forms:

Amaranth: a journal of food writing and art: "Grasped"
Atticus Review: "Broken"
Clade Song: "Crickets"
Ecozon@: "Fiddlehead feint," "Fiddlehead tonic," "Ghost bowing," and "Spiral"
Gyroscope Review: "Mouth Art of the Bald-faced Hornet"
The Hopper: Environmental Lit. Poetry. Art.: "Worm sex"
Lammergeier Magazine: "Seized"
Minnow Literary Magazine: "Flight"
New Croton Review: "Rapture: early lessons"
Northern Appalachian Review: "Ephemera" and "Snow-melt carrion call"
Notre Dame Review: "Amphibious"
The Rumen: "It looks like rage" and "Cicada courtship"
Snapdragon Journal: "Flood"
Split Rock Review: "Sanctuary"
Stone Canoe: "Beech"

A chapbook also entitled *Mouth Art of the Bald-faced Hornet* was a finalist in the 2022 Kingdoms in the Wild Annual Poetry Prize. "Broken" was awarded first prize in the Modern Sonnet category in the Helen Schaible 2022 International Sonnet Contest Awards. "Mouth Art of the Bald-faced Hornet" was nominated for a Pushcart Prize.

Many thanks to Swarthmore College for a sabbatical leave that allowed me to draft these poems. Still greater thanks to Dilruba Ahmed, Nathalie Anderson, and Ann Aspell for careful guidance through many stages of revision—as well as to Leah Huete de Maines, publisher of Finishing Line Press, for selecting the manuscript, and to Christen Kincaid for careful and patient editing. Almost all of these poems are set in the occupied and unceded lands of Lenapehoking: I am grateful beyond words for Indigenous people who cared for these lands and for the wood and water communities that remain. I have learned so much about the woods from my colleagues on the Crum Woods Stewardship Committee, especially Jeff Jabco, Roger Latham, Claire Sawyers, Art McGarity, José-Luis Machado, Lars Rasmussen. I have taken other lessons from my long-standing colleagues in English literature (Rachel Buurma, Lara Cohen, Anthony Foy, Nora Johnson, Baki Mani, Chinelo Okparanta, Gina Patnaik, Peter Schmidt, Val Smith, Eric Song, and Craig Williamson) and Environmental Studies (Adrienne Benally, Tim Burke, Giovanna Di Chiro, Peter Collings, Carr Everbach, Chris Graves, Eric Jensen, Carol Nackenoff, Jennifer Peck, Jennifer Pfluger, Christy Schuetze, and Mark Wallace), as well as David Cohen, whose aesthetic sophistication disproves Whitman's learned astronomer. Students in my Poetry and Writing Nature workshops have indulged and shared my delight in the lyricism of the woods. Chara Armon, Nino Campobasso,

Andrea Liu, and Doug Durian have been fellow-walkers in the woods and in life. John, Sara, and Nathan Posey-Alston bring music and joy. Rachel Pastan and Nancy Neiman have been boon companions through more than I could have imagined. Jim, Doug, and Kristen Bolton show up every week. James, Zoë, and Jeremy Peyton Jones have paddled, walked, waited, ice-slid, and rock-climbed through the years with me. To all, many thanks.

Betsy Bolton is a poet, a digital storyteller, and professor of English and Environmental Studies. Her poetry has appeared in reviews such as T*he Hopper, Gyroscope, Split Rock, Notre Dame,* and *Ecozon@,* and has been nominated for a Pushcart Prize. She teaches at Swarthmore College, on Lenape land, at the boundary between the Piedmont and the Coastal Plain. These poems are in conversation with the Crum creek and woods and the communities embedded and fostered there. This is her first book of poetry.

Bolton served as a Fulbright scholar to Morocco in 2013-14. As a counterpoint to the then-prevailing sensationalism of North American writings about Morocco, she facilitated the creation of digital stories (short, autobiographical videos) to highlight the varied experiences of different groups of Moroccan citizens: teachers in remote areas of the High Atlas mountains, students at an elite, English-language university, and traditional craftsmen in the Fès medina. These stories can be found at maghrebi-voices.swarthmore.edu. In 2017-18, as a Fulbrighter to Bhutan, Betsy helped establish the country's first short-lived MA program in English literature; she again facilitated digital storytelling and filmed miniature documentaries of traditional crafts. This work can be found at the-great-happiness.swarthmore.edu.

In addition to her creative work, Bolton is the author of *Women, Nationalism, and the Romantic Stage: Theatre and Politics, 1780-1800* (Cambridge University Press, 2001). A new book, *In the Kingdom of the Thunder Dragon: Happiness, History, and Environment in a Changing Bhutan,* is forthcoming with Lever Press.

www.ingramcontent.com/pod-product-compliance
Lightning Source LLC
Chambersburg PA
CBHW020338170426
43200CB00006B/423